The Great Historical Forgeries Upon Which Papal Authority Is Founded

By
JOHANN JOSEPH IGNAZ VON DOELLINGER
ROMAN CATHOLICISM'S GREATEST HISTORIAN

Introduction By
EMMETT MCLOUGHLIN

ISBN: 978-2-925611-02-8
Printed in the USA.

INTRODUCTION

Christians feel that the Christian Church and its traditions are founded upon the New Testament of the Bible. Protestants think that the ultimate authority ends there — in the Bible.

Roman Catholics are likewise taught that the Roman Catholic Church is based upon the Bible, principally upon the New Testament. They believe, also, that those Biblical injunctions, especially "Thou art Peter and upon this rock I will found My Church," are to be explained as the early Christian saintly thinkers, "the Fathers" felt they should be. This "tradition" of early century theologians becomes as "inspired" and infallible as the Bible itself.

Hence the Catechism says the infallible doctrine of the true Church rests upon Scripture and Tradition.

The "doctrine" of the Catholic Church includes the "authority" of its leaders, both spiritual and political.

The Scriptures, i.e. the New Testament, say nothing of the political and territorial authority of the Church's head, the Pope of Rome.

To fill this gap in the power and authority of the bishops of Rome — the Popes, there has been developed through several centuries the most fantastic framework of forged documents that the world has ever dreamed of. This is a real life fantasy of lies and perjury that makes the world's historical liars, thieves and baronial robbers the most childish of amateurs.

That all of these century spanning lies should be done in the name of Christ's religion is shocking. That the Roman Catholic Church should have used these forged documents as the foundatioin of its authority is appalling. That the Vatican's present title to the land it rests upon is based upon proven false title is unconscionable. That its extensioin of power and authority over a half billion Christians around the world is resting upon a non existent foundation, Scriptural or political, is a phenonenom more unbelievable than the story of the lost continent of Atlantis.

One of the soundest of Roman Catholic historians was Rev. Johann Joseph Ignaz Von Doellinger. He clashed headon with the Jesuit political and theological historians during the preliminaries and the main event of the First Vatican Council of 1870.

The Jesuits backed Pope Pius IX for Papal Infallibility. For them it meant political infallibility.

The priest theologian fought for Papal integrity, instead of Papal infallibility.

He demonstrated in the process that Papal claims to territorial domains and to political authority were not only a very gradual development within the Vatican but they rested upon completely false and forged documents.

The most glaring of these documents is the "Donation of Constantine." Constantine was the Roman Emperor in the fourth century. The document of the "Donation" was forged in the eighth century. According to it, Constantine, in gratitude to Pope Silvester for his cure from leprosy, gave the Pope Italy and other lands, as well as authority over the patriarchates of Jerusalem, Antioch, Alexandria and Constantinople.

The further astounding fact is that Catholic historians at the time of Pope Pius IX admitted that the "Donation of Constantine" was a false document but Pius still claimed sovereignty over the Papal States.

The Vatican position now is the same as that of a man admitting that his title to his home is clouded or false but still contending that the house is his because he is living in it.

The "Donation of Constantine" is only one of a ream of fabulous forgeries described by Doellinger in the following exerpt from his book "The Pope and the Council," published in 1869.

The imaginative boldness of the churchmen who concocted these forgeries is exceeded only by the boldness of the modern churchmen who still claim the power while admitting that the documents upon which it is based are false.

Before reading the text of Johann Von Doellinger's exposition of the forgeries that are the foundation of the Vatican, it might be well to consider the modern claims of the Pope as expressed on the title page of the U. S. Official Catholic Directory for 1964:

"HIS HOLINESS THE POPE, BISHOP OF ROME AND VICAR OF JESUS CHRIST, SUCCESSOR OF ST. PETER, PRINCE OF THE APOSTLES, SUPREME PONTIFF OF THE UNIVERSAL CHURCH, PATRIARCH OF THE WEST, PRIMATE OF ITALY, ARCHBISHOP AND METROPOLITAN OF THE ROMAN PROVINCE, SOVEREIGN OF VATICAN CITY.

Emmett McLoughlin

Phoenix, Arizona

FORGERIES

At the beginning of the ninth century no change had taken place in the constitution of the Church as we have described it, and especially none as to the authority for deciding matters of faith. When the Frankish bishops came to Leo III., he assured them that, far from setting himself above the Fathers of the Council in 381, who made the additions to the Nicene Creed, he did not venture to put himself on a par with them, and therefore refused to sanction the interpolation of *Filioque* into the Creed.[1]

But in the middle of that century — about 845 — arose the huge fabrication of the Isidorian decretals, which had results far beyond what its author contemplated, and gradually, but surely, changed the whole constitution and government of the Church. It would be difficult to find in all history a second instance of so successful, and yet so clumsy a forgery. For three centuries past it has been exposed, yet the principles it introduced and brought into practice have taken such deep root in the soil of the Church, and have so grown into her life, that the exposure of the fraud has produced no result in shaking the dominant system.

About a hundred pretended decrees of the earliest Popes, together with certain spurious writings of other Church dignitaries and acts of Synods, were then fabricated in the west of Gaul, and eagerly seized upon by Pope Nicolas I. at Rome, to be used as genuine documents in support of the new claims put forward by himself and his successors. The immediate object of the compiler of this forgery was to protect bishops against their metropolitans and other authorities, so as to secure absolute impunity, and the exclusion of all influence of the secular power. This end was to be gained through such an immense extension of the Papal power, that, as these principles gradually penetrated the Church, and were followed out into their consequences, she necessarily assumed the form of an absolute monarchy subjected to the arbitrary power of a single individual, and the foundation of the edifice of Papal Infallibility was already laid — first, by the principle that the decrees of every Council require Papal confirmation; secondly, by the assertion that the fulness of power, even in matters of faith, resides in the Pope alone, who is bishop of the universal Church, while the other bishops are his servants.

Now, if the Pope is really the bishop of the whole Church, so that every other bishop is his servant, he, who is the sole and

---

1 *Concil. Gall.* (ed. Sirmondi) ii. 256.

legitimate mouth of the Church, ought to be infallible. If the decrees of Councils are invalid without Papal confirmation, the divine attestation of a doctrine undeniably rests in the last resort on the word of one man, and the notion of the absolute power of that one man over the whole Church includes that of his infallibility, as the shell contains the kernel. With perfect consistency, therefore, the pseudo-Isidore makes his early Popes say: "The Roman Church remains to the end free from stain of heresy."[1]

Formerly all learned students of ecclesiastical antiquity and canon-law — men like De Marca, Baluze, Coustant, Gilbert, Berardi, Zallwein, etc. — were agreed that the change introduced by the pseudo-Isidore was a substantial one, that it displaced the old system of Church government and brought in the new. Modern writers have maintained that the compiler of the forgery only meant to codify the existing state of things, and give it a formal status, and that the same development would have taken place without his trick.[2] The truth is:—

First, Before his fabrication many very efficacious forgeries had won a gradual recognition at Rome since the beginning of the sixth century; and on them was based the maxim that the Pope, as supreme in the Church, could be judged by no man.

Secondly, The Isidorian doctrine contradicted itself, for it aimed at two things which were mutually incompatible, — the complete independence and impunity of bishops on the one hand, and the advancement of Papal power on the other. The first point it sought to effect by such strange and unpractical rules that they never attained any real vitality, while, on the contrary, the principles about the power of the Roman See worked their way, and became dominant under favourable circumstances, but with a result greatly opposed to the views of Isidore, by bringing the bishops into complete subjection to Rome. But that the pseudo-Isidorian principles eventually revolutionized the whole constitution of the Church, and introduced a new system in place of the old, — on that point there can be no controversy among candid hisitorians.

At the time when the forged decretals began to be widely known, the See of Rome was occupied by Nicolas I. (858-867), a Pope who exceeded all his predecessors in the audacity of his designs.

---

1 *Ep. Lucii* in Hinschius' ed. of Decretals, p. 179. Cf. p. 206 The same statement is put into the mouth of Marcus and Felix I.

2 So Walter, Phillips, Schulte, Pachmann, among canonists, and Dollinger in his *Church History* (ii. 41-43), on grounds betraying a very imperfect knowledge of the decretals.

Favoured and protected by the break-up of the empire of Charles the Great, he met East and West alike with the firm resolution of pressing to the uttermost every claim of any one of his predecessors, and pushing the limits of the Roman supremacy to the point of absolute monarchy. By a bold but non-natural torturing of a single word against the sense of a whole code of law, he managed to give a turn to a canon of a General Council, excluding all appeals to Rome, as though it opened to the whole clergy in East and West a right of appeal to Rome, and made the Pope the supreme judge of all bishops and clergy of the whole world.[1] He wrote this to the Eastern Emperor, to the Frankish king, Charles, and to all the Frankish bishops.[2] And he referred the Orientals, and so sharp-sighted a man as Photius, to those fabrications fathered on Popes Silvester and Sixtus, which were thenceforth used for centuries, and gained the Roman Church the oft-repeated reproach from the Greeks, of being the native home of inventions and falsifications of documents. Soon after, receiving the new implements forged in the Isidorian workshop (about 863 or 864), Nicolas met the doubts of the Frankish bishops with the assurance that the Roman Church had long preserved all those documents with honour in her archives, and that every writing of a Pope, even if not part of the Dionysian collection of canons, was binding on the whole Church.[3] In a Synod at Rome in 863 he had accordingly anathematized all who should refuse to receive the teaching or ordinances of a Pope.[4] If, indeed, all Papal utterances were a rule for the whole Church, and all decrees of Councils dependent on the Pope's good pleasure, — as Nicolas asserted on the strength of the Isidorian forgery, — then there would be but one step further to the promulgation of Papal Infallibility, though it has been long delayed. It was thought enough to repeat from time to time that the Roman Church keeps the faith pure, and is free from every stain.

Nearly three centuries passed before the seed sown produced its full harvest. For almost two hundred years, from the death of Nicolas I. to the time of Leo IX., the Roman See was in a condition which did not allow of any systematic acquisition and enforcement of new or extended rights. For above sixty years

---

1 Canon 17 of Chalcedon, which speaks of appeals to the "primas dioceseos," *i.e.*, one of the Eastern patriarchs, not a civil ruler, as Baxmann thinks (*Politik der Pabste*, ii. 13). Nicolas said the singular meant the plural "dioceseon," and that the "primate" meant the Pope,—a notion which would not seem worth a reply in Constantinople.
2 Mansi, *Concil.* i, 202, 688, 694.
3 Mansi, *Concil.* xv. 695.
4 Harduin, *Concil.* v. 574.

(883-955) the Roman Church was enslaved and degraded, while the Apostolic See became the prey and the plaything of rival factions of the nobles, and for a long time of ambitious and profligate women. It was only renovated for a brief interval (997-1003) in the persons of Gregory V. and Silvester II., by the influence of the Saxon emperor. Then the Papacy sank back into utter confusion and moral impotence; the Tuscan Counts made it hereditary in their family; again and again dissolute boys, like John XII. and Benedict IX., occupied and disgraced the Apostolic throne, which was now bought and sold like a piece of merchandise, and at last three Popes fought for the tiara, until the Emperor Henry III. put an end to the scandal by elevating a German bishop to the See of Rome.

With Leo IX. (1048-1054) was inaugurated a new era of the Papacy, which may be called the Hildebrandine. Within sixty years, through the contest with kings, bishops, and clergy, against simony, clerical marriage, and investiture, the Roman See had risen to a height of power even Nicolas I. never aspired to. A large and powerful party, stronger than that which two hundred years before had undertaken to carry through the Isidorian forgery, had been labouring since the middle of the eleventh century, with all its might, to weld the States of Europe into a theocratic priest-kingdom, with the Pope as its head. The urgent need of reform in the Church helped on the growth of the spiritual monarchy, and again the purification of the Church seemed to need such a concentration and increase of ecclesiastical power. In France this party was supported by the most influential spiritual corporation of the time, the Congregation of Cluny. In Italy, men like Peter Damiani, Bishop Anselm of Lucca, Humbert, Deusdedit, and above all Hildebrand, — who was the life and soul of the enterprise, — helped on the new system, though some of them, as Damiani and Hildebrand, differed widley both in theory and practice.

It has not perhaps been sufficiently observed that Gregory VII. is in fact the only one of all the Popes who set himself with clear and deliberate purpose to introduce a new constitution of the Church, and by new means. He regarded himself not merely as the reformer of the Church, but as the divinely commissioned founder of a wholly new order of things, fond as he was of appealing to his predecessors. Nicolas I. alone approaches him in this, but none of the later Popes, all of whom, even the boldest, have but filled in the outline he sketched.

Gregory saw from the first that Synods regularly held by the Popes, and new codes of Church law, were the means for introducing the new system. Synods had been held, at his suggestion, by Leo IX. and his successors, and he himself carried on the work in those assembled after 1073. But only Popes and their legates were henceforth to hold Synods; in every other form the institution was to disappear. Gregory collected about him by degrees the right men for elaborating his system of Church law. Anselm of Lucca, nephew of Pope Alexander II., compiled the most important and comprehensive work, at his command, between 1080 and 1086. Anselm may be called the founder of the new Gregorian system of Church law, first, by extracting and putting into convenient working shape everything in the Isidorian forgeries serviceable for the Papal absolutism; next, by altering the law of the Church, through a tissue of fresh inventions and interpolations, in accordance with the requirements of his party and the stand-point of Gregory.[1] Then came Deusdedit, whom Gregory made a Cardinal, with some more inventions. At the same time Bonizo compiled his work, the main object of which was to exalt the Papal prerogatives. The forty propositions or titles of this part of his work correspond entirely to Gregory's *Dictatus* and the materials supplied by Anselm and Deusdedit.[2] The last great work of the Gregorians (before Gratian) was the *Polycarpus* of Cardinal Gregory of Pavia (before 1118), which almost always adheres to Anselm in its falsifications.[3]

The Preface of Deusdedit to his work is the programme of the whole school whose labours were at length crowned with such complete success.[4] The Roman Church, says the Cardinal, is the mother of all Churches, for Peter first founded the Patriarchal Sees of the East, and then gave bishops to all the cities of the West. Councils cannot be held without the sanction of the Pope, according to the decisions of the 318 Fathers at Nice. The Roman clergy rule without the Pope, when the See is vacant, and therefore Cyprian and the Africans humbly submitted to their decisions before the election of Cornelius—a pet crotchet of the Cardinal's,

---

1 The contents of the Anselmian collection are known from the list of chapters in the *Spicilegium Rom.* (ed. Mai, vi.); from Antonius Augustinus, *Epitome Juris Pontif.* (Paris, 1641); and from the citations of Pithou in the Paris edition of Gratian, 1686.

2 *Nova Patrum Biblioth.* (ed. Mai), vii. 3, 48.

3 Ivo of Chartres, though a contemporary of Cardinal Gregory, cannot be reckoned among the Gregorian canonists. Much as he was influenced in his compilations by Isidore, and sometimes by Anselm, still in certain important articles he held to the old Church law.

4 It is found in *Memorie del Card. Passionei* (Roma, 1762), p. 30.

which Anselm, who was not a Cardinal, did not adopt. He adds, that he writes in order to confirm the authority of Rome and the liberty of the Church against its assailants, and maintains that the testimonies he has collected disprove all objections, on the principle that the lesser must always yield to the greater—*i.e.*, the authority of Councils and Fathers to the Pope. With this one axiom—which not only opened the door wide for the Isidorian decretals, but prevented any attempt to moderate their system by an appeal to the ancient canons—the revolution in the Church was accomplished in the simplest and least troublesome manner.

Clearly and cautiously as the Gregorian party went to work, they lived in a world of dreams and illusions about the past and about remote countries. They could not escape the imperative necessity of demonstrating their new system to have been the constant practice of the Church, and it is difficult, if not impossible, to distinguish where involuntary delusion merged into conscious deceit. Whatever present exigencies required was selected from the mythical stores at their command hastily and recklessly; then fresh inventions were added, and soon every claim of Rome could be shown to have a legitimate foundation in existing records and decrees.

It is so far true to say, that without the pseudo-Isidore there would have been no Gregory vii., that the Isidorian forgeries were the broad foundation the Gregorians built upon. But the first object of Isidore was to secure the impunity of bishops, whereas the Roman party—which for a long time had a majority of the bishops against it—wanted to introduce a state of things where the Popes or their legates could summarily depose bishops, intimidate them, and reduce them to complete subjection to every Papal command. The newly invented doctrines about the deposing power contributed to this end. In a word, a new history and a new civil and canon law was required, and both had to be obtained by improving on the Isidorian principles with new forgeries. The correction of history was to some extent provided for in Germany by the monk Bernold, and in Italy by the zealous Gregorian Bonizo, Bishop of Piacenza, who tried, among other things, to get rid of the coronatiion of Charles the Great.[1] Their other assistants had to invent or adapt historical facts for party purposes, for their new codes of Church law innovated largely on ancient Church history. Gregory himself had his own little stock of fabricated or

---

1 See Jaffe's Introduction to his edition of Bonitho in *Monumenta Gregor.*, pp. 596 *seq.*

distorted facts to support pretensions and undertakings which seemed to his contemporaries strange and unauthorized. It was, for instance, an axiomatic fact with him that Pope Innocent I. excommunicated the Emperor Arcadius, that Pope Zachary deposed the Frankish king Childeric, and that Gregory the Great threatened to depose the kings who should rob a hospice at Autun.[1] He treated the Donation of Constantine as a valuable and important document; it gave him a right over Corsica and Sardinia. His pupil Leo IX. used it against the Greeks, and his friend Peter Damiani against Germany; Anslem and Deusdedit assigned it a prominent place in their legal books.

At the same time, Gregory thought it most important, with all his legislative activity and lofty claims and high-handed measures, not to seem too much of an innovator and despot; he constantly affirmed that he only wished to restore the ancient laws of the Church, and abolish late abuses. When he drew out the whole system of Papal omnipotence in twenty-seven theses in his *Dictatus,* these theses were partly mere repetitions or corollaries of the Isidorian decretals; partly he and his friends and allies sought to give them the appearance of tradition and antiquity by new fictions.[2]

Gregory's chief work is his letter to Bishop Hermann of Metz, designed to prove how well grounded is the Pope's dominion over emperors and kings, and his right to depose them in cases of necessity. In this he showed his adherents how to manipulate facts and texts, by twisting a passage in a letter of Pope Gelasius to the Emperor Anastasius so skilfully, by means of omissions and arbitrary collocations, as to make Gelasius say just the opposite of what he really said,—viz., that kings are absolutely and universally subject to the Pope, whereas what he did say was, that rulers of the Church are always subject to the laws of the emperors, only disclaiming the interference of the secular power in questions of faith and the sacraments.[3]

How what was a falsification to begin with was falsified again in the interests of the new system, and accentuated to serve the

---

1 He appealed to a recently forged document in Autun, which Launoi ▲*Opp.* v. p. ii. 445) has dissected.

2 As to this *Dictatus* being his own work, and an authentic part of the Register edited by himself, see Giesebrecht, *Gesetzgeb. der Rom. Kirche., Munchner hist. Jahrbuch,* 1866, p. 149.

3 *Registr.* (ed. Jaffe), p. 457.

cause of ecclesiastical despotism, may be seen from the eleventh canon of *Causa* 25, Q. 1, in Gratian. The Council of Toledo in 646 had excommunicated the Spanish priests who took part in the rebellion against the King, and included the King himself in the anathema if he violated this censure *(hujus canonis censuram)*. Out of this Isidore made, two hundred years afterwards, the following:—The anathema applied to all kings who violated any canon binding under censure, or allowed it to be violated by others; and this he put into the mouth of Pope Hadrian.[1] In the new text-books compiled by Anselm, Deusdedit, and Gregory of Pavia, *the (pretended) decrees of the Popes were put in place of the canons of Councils,* and this supplied just what was wanted— a system of ancient Church law to justify the procedures of Gregory VII. and Urban II. against the princes of their own day —and a Pope would never lack some pretext for threatening excommunication, with all its consequences.[2]

Gregory borrowed one main pillar of his system from the False Decretals. Isidore had made Pope Julius (about 338) write to the Eastern bishops,—"The Church of Rome, by a singular privilege, has the right of opening and shutting the gates of heaven to whom she will."[3] On this Gregory built his scheme of dominion.[4] How should not he be able to judge on earth, on whose will hung the salvation or damnation of men? The passage was made into a special decree or chapter in the new codes.[5] *The typical formula of binding and loosing had become an inexhaustible treasure-chamber of rights and claims.* The Gregorians used it as a charm to put them in possession of everything worth having. If Gregory —who was notoriously the first to undertake dethroning kings— wanted to depose the German Emperor, he said, "To me is given power to bind and loose on earth and in heaven."[6] Were subjects to be absolved from their oaths of allegiance?—which he was also the first to attempt,—he did it by virtue of his power to loose. Did he want to dispose of other people's property? he declared, as at his Roman Synod of 1080,—"We desire to show the world that we can give or take away at our will kingdoms, duchies,

---

1 *Capp, Angilram.* p. 769 (ed. Hinsch.)

2 The monk Bernold, in his *Apol. contr. Schismat.*, written in 1087 (Ussermann, ed. p. 361), fabricates "Apostolicae Sedis statuta."

3 *Decret. pseudo-Is.* (ed. Hinsch.), p. 464.

4 *Monum, Gregor.* (ed. Jaffe), p. 445.

5 By Deusdedit; see *Galland, Syll.* ii. 745; by Anselm, *Maii Spicil. Rom.* vi. 317, 23; by Bonizo, *Maii Pat. Nov. Biblioth.* vii. 3, 47; Gregory's *Polycarpus,* i. 4, tit. 34.

6 See the form in Mansi, xx. 467.

earldoms, in a word, the possessions of all men; for we can bind and loose."[1] In the same way a saying ascribed to Constantine, at the Council of Nice, in a legend recorded by Rufinus, was amplified till it was fashioned into a perfect mine of high-flying pretensions. Constantine, according to this fable, when the written accusations of the bishops against each other were laid before him, burned them, saying, in allusion to a verse of the Psalter, that the bishops were gods, and no man could dare to judge them. Nicolas I. quoted this to the Emperor Michael.[2] Anselm adopted the story into his collection, Gratian followed, and Gregory himself found in it clear evidence that he, the Pope, the bishop of bishops, stood in unapproachable majesty over all monarchs of the earth. For, as the passage stood in Anslem and Gratian, it was the Pope whom Constantine called a god, and so it has been understood and explained ever since.[3]

A man like Gregory VII., little familiar as he was with theological questions, must have held the prerogative of Infallibility the most precious jewel of his crown. His claims to universal dominion, to the deposing power, and the right of dispensing subjects from their oaths, all rested ultimately on his own authority. All was to be believed because he, the infallible Pope, affirmed it. Accordingly, stronger proofs and testimonies than Isidore supplied had to be found for this infallibility of his.

Pope Agatho had said at a Roman Synod, in 680, that all the English bishops were to observe the ordinances made in former Roman Synods for the Anglo-Saxon Church.[4] Cardinal Deusdedit made this into a decree issued by Agatho to all bishops in the world, saying they must receive all Papal orders as though attested by the very voice of Peter, and therefore, of course, infallible.[5] One of the boldest falsifications the Gregorians allowed themselves occurs first in Anslem's[6] and then in Cardinal Gregory's works, from whom Gratian borrowed it. St. Augustine had said that all those canonical writings (of the Bible) were pre-eminently

---

1 Mansi, xx. 536, "Quia si potestis in coelo ligare et solvere, potestis in terra imperia . . . et omnium hominum possessiones pro meritis tollere unicuique et concedere."

2 Mansi, xv. 215.

3 *Dist.* 96, 97. "Satis evidenter ostenditur a saeculari potestate nec ligari prorsus nec solvi posse *Pontificem, quem constat a pio Principe Constantino Deum appellatum,* nec posse deum ab hominibus judicari manifestum est."

4 Labbe, *Concil.* vi. 580.

5 It occurs in the same spurious form in Gregory's *Polycarpus,* Ivo's Collection, and—which was, of course, quite conclusive—in Gratian's *Decretum,* Dist. 19, c. 2.

6 See Pithou's ed. of Gratian. Cf. Grat. *Dist.* 19, c. 6.

attested, which Apostolical Churches had first received and possessed. He meant the Churches of Corinth, Ephesus, etc. The passage was corrupted into,—"Those Epistles belong to canonical writings which the Holy See has issued;" and thus it came to pass that the mediaeval theologians and canonists, who generally derived their whole knowledge of the Fathers from the passages collected by Peter Lombard and Gratian, really believed that St. Augustine had put the decretal letters of Popes on a par with Scripture.[1] When Cardinal Turrecremata, about 1450, and Cardinal Cajetan, about 1516, put the Infallibility doctrine into formal shape, they too relied on the clear testimony of St. Augustine, which left no doubt that the first theologian of the ancient Church had declared every Papal utterance to be as free from error as the Apostolical Epistles.[2]

That Papal Infallibility might be more firmly believed, *personal sanctity* was also ascribed to every Pope. This notion was first invented by Ennodius, deacon and secretary of Pope Symmachus, who wrote in 503 to defend him against certain charges. The Popes, he said, must be held to inherit innocence and sanctity from Peter.[3] Isidore eagerly seized on this, and *invented two* Roman Synods, which had unanimously approved and subscribed the work of Ennodius.[4] Gregory VII. made this holiness of all Popes, which he said he had personal experience of, the foundation of his claim to universal dominion.[5] Every sovereign, he said, however good before, becomes corrupted by the use of power, whereas every rightly appointed Pope[6] becomes a saint through the imputed merits of St. Peter. Even an exorcist[7] among the clergy, he added, is higher and more powerful than every secular monarch, for he casts out devils, whose slaves evil princes are. This doctrine of the personal sanctity of every Pope, put forward by the Gregorians, and by Gregory VII. himself, as a claim made by Pope Symmachus, was adopted into the codes of canon law. But as notorious facts, and the crimes and excesses of many Popes, which no denials could get rid of, were in glar-

---

1 The title of the canon in Gratian is "Inter canoniicas Scripturas decretales epistolae annumerantur."

2 Turrecremata, *Summa de Eccl.* P. ii.; Cajetan, *De Primat. Rom.* c. 14. Alphonsus de Castro has exposed the whole forgery in his work *Adv. Hoeres.* (Paris, 1565) i. 11.

3 *Liber Apol., Opp.* (Sirmondi) i. 1921.

4 *Decret. pseudo-Isidor.* (ed. Hinsch.), pp. 675, *seq.*

5 *Ep.* viii, 21 (*Jaffeq*, p. 463.

6 This proviso was meant to cover the frequent caases of such evil Popes as *e.g.*, John XII, and Benedict IX.

7 [One of the lower ranks of the Catholic clergy.—Tr.]

ing contradiction to it, a supplementary theory had to be invented, which Cardinal Deusdedit published under the venerated name of St. Boniface, the apostle of Germany. It was to this effect:— *Even if a Pope is so bad that he drags down whole nations to hell with him in troops, nobody can rebuke him; for he who judges all can be judged of no man;* the only exception is in case of his swerving from the faith. That this could have been written nowhere but in Rome, and certainly not by St. Boniface, is self-evident. There were no "innumerable nations" in his day for the Pope to drag down into hell with him like slaves. The words imply past experience of many profligate Popes, and a period of enormously extended Papal power over the nations, and were clearly invented after the pontificate of Benedict IX. Gratian has, of course, adopted them from Deusdedit.[1]

The Gregorian doctrine since 1080 then is, that every Pope, lawfully appointed, and not thrust in by force, is holy and infallible. But his holiness is imputed, not inherent, so that if he have no merits of his own, he inherits those of his predecessor St. Peter. Notwithstanding his holiness, he may drag countless troops of men down to hell, and none of them may withstand or warn him; notwithstanding his infallibility, he may become an apostate, and then he may be resisted. Probably the later distinction between his official *ex cathedra* infallibility and his personal denial of the faith was implied here.

Gregory VII. seems to have sincerely believed that his infallibility was already acknowledged throughout the Christian world, even in the East. He wrote to the Emperor Henry, "The Greek Church is fallen away, and the Armenians also have lost the right faith, but," he adds, "all the Easterns await from St. Peter (viz., from me) the decision on their various opinions, and at this time will the promise of Peter's confirming his brethren be fulfilled."[1] He wanted then (in 1074) to go at the head of a great army to Constantinople, and there to hold his solemn judgment in matters of faith, for he does not seem to have counted on the voluntary submission of the Greeks; instead of which he contented himself with plunging Germany and Italy into a religious and civil war, the end of which he did not live to see. All history proves, he says, how clearly holiness is connected with infallibility in the Popes. While there are at most only a few kings or emperors who have been holy, out of 153 Popes 100 have not only been

1 *Dist.* 40, c. 53.
2 *Ep.* ii. 31, p. 45 (Jaffe).

holy, but have reached the highest grade of sanctity.[1] And the Gregorians desseminated the fable, which even the well-known annals of the Popes contradicted, that of the thirty before Constantine all be one were martyrs.[2] The Gregorians busied themselves with the rectification of Papal history, and as the apostasy of Liberius—copied from St. Jerome's Chronicle into so many historical works—was not easy to reconcile with Papal infallibility and sanctity, Anslem, adopted into his codex the earlier fable, that Liberius, when exiled, had ordained Felix his successor, by advice of the Roman clergy, and abdicated, so that his subsequent apostasy did not matter.[3]

If every Pope is holy and infallible, then, according to the Gregorian view, all Christendom must tremble before him, as before an Asiatic despot whose disfavour is death. Accordingly, Anselm and Cardinal Gregory extracted passages from older forgeries, especially from a spurious speech of St. Peter, to the effect that no one should hold intercourse with a man under the Pope's displeasure.[4] *Like the successive strata of the earth covering one another, so layer after layer of forgeries and fabrications was piled up in the Church.* This shows itself most conspicuously in the great Church question of Synods, where the two contradictory views of the self-government and administration of the Church by Councils, and of the absolute sovereignty of the Pope and Court of Rome over the whole Church, were at issue. In 342, Pope Julius had written to the Eastern Bishops, who had confirmed the deposition of St. Athanasius at the Synod of Antioch, that they should not have acted for themselves in a matter affectiing the whole Church, but, according to ecclesiastical custom, in union with "all of us," *i.e.*, the bishops of the West.[5] Socrates, who welcomed an opportunity of pointing out the ambition of the Roman Church,[6] had twisted this into Julius saying that nothing could be decided without the bishop of Rome. His Latin translator, Epiphanius the Italian, about 500, went a step further, and made the Pope say that no Council could be held without his consent.[7] Isidore worked up these materials, and made Pope

---

1 *Ep.* viii. 21, p. 463 (Jaffe).

2 Bonizo, *Patr. Nov. Bibl.* vii. 3, 37 (ed. Mai).

3 Schelstrate (*Antiq. Illustr.* i. 456) quotes the passage from Anselm.

4 See Gratian, *Dist.* 93, c. i.

5 *Ep. Rom. Pont.* (ed. Coustant), p. 386.

6 Thus he observes (vii. 11) that the Roman See, like the Alexandrian, had for some time advanced to dominion (dunasteia) over the priesthood.

7 *Hist. Trip, i,* D, T.

Julius write, in two spurious epistles, that the Apostles and the Nicene Council had said no Council could be held without the Pope's injunction. And thus Anselm and the other Gregorian canonists could quote a whole string of primitive decrees resting Councils and all their decisions on the arbitration of the Pope, and Gratian has borrowed the whole of his seventeenth Distinction from Anselm.

Even this was not enough. Not only were Councils to be made dependent, but the institution itself, as it had existed for nine hundred years, was to be abolished. As the kings who had become absolute in the sixteenth and seventeenth centuries could no longer endure any representative assemblies, so the Papacy, when it wished to become absolute, found that Synods of particular National Churches were better out of the way altogether. For it was only in and by means of Synods of particular districts, provinces, and National Churches, that a healthy and somewhat independent Church life could spread and maintain itself. These had therefore to be put an end to, or at least broken up and made so difficult that they could only proceed at the beck of Rome. The following forgery was used for the purpose:—

The opponents of Pope Symmachus, in 503, in order to show that they could assemble in Rome without him, had affirmed that the annual Provincial Synods prescribed by the Church would not lose their force merely because the Pope was not present at them. Ennodius, in his defence of Symmachus, replied that weighty causes *(causae majores)* were by the canon of Sardica reserved to the Pope. That was itself a misrepresentation, long current in Rome; the canon only gave a right of appeal to Rome for bishops. Anselm of Lucca, and Cardinal Gregory, and Gratian after him, made out of this the following decree of Pope Symmachus—"The Provincial Councils ordered by the canons to be held annually, have lost their validity from the Pope not being present at them." And the title of the decree is, "Provincial Synods without the Pope's presence have no force" *(pondere carent)*.[1] And thus an ecclesiastical revolution was brought about in three lines.

But a formal prohibition of all Synods was still wanted, and this was attained by Anselm, Cardinal Gregory and Gratian after them, making Pope Gregory the Great declare that no one ever had been, or ever would be, permitted to hold a particular (not

---

[1] *Dist,* 17, c. 6.

CEcumenical) Synod.[1] The fraud lay in converting what Pelagius I. had said, in the particular case of the schism of Aquileia, of a Council assembled against the Fifth CEcumenical, into a general prohibition issued by Gregory I. against all Synods, while, by changing the plural into the singular, a reference to the authority of the Apostolic Churches of Alexandria and Antioch was altered into an exaltation of Papal authority.[2] And thus the double end was attained of putting down all meetings of bishops as in itself an illegal act of presumption, and at the same time bringing out prominently the plenitude of the Papal power, which could even withdraw from all Christendom the apostolical institution of Synods at its will.

But Isidore's chief contribution to the designs of Gregory VII. was by his *inventions about the effect of excommunication*, for this, in the extended sense given it by Gregory, was the sharpest weapon in the struggle for Papal domination. Isidore had made the earliest Popes assert that no speech ever could be held with an excommunicated man, whence Gregory and his allies inferred that *this applied also to kings and emperors, and that nobody could, even in matters of business, hold any intercourse with them if excommunicated, so that they were no longer fit to reign, and must be deposed.* By this extension of the idea, wholly unknown to the ancient Church, and destructive of the entire original character of the institution, an enormous instrument of power was created, which not only might be abused, but was itself a standing abuse, a confusion of things human and divine, and a perpetual source of civil disturbance and division. Bossuet has admitted that it was a false doctrine which Gregory introduced into the Church, by altering and distorting the notion of excommunication.[3] Gregory himself must have known he was the first to make the claim, and that even in the Isidorian decretals there was nothing like it, yet at the Synod of 1078[4] he grounded it exclusively on the statutes of his predecessors. To make their spiritual arms irresistible, the Gregorians also borrowed from Isidore an alleged rule of Pope Urban I., addressed to all bishops, that even an unjust excommunication by a bishop must be respected, and nobody could receive the condemned man.[5]

---

1 *Decret. Dist.* 17, c. 4.

2 Cf. on this and other falsifications, Berardi, *Gratian. Can.* ii. 489.

3 *Defens. Declar.* para. 1. 1. 8. c. 7.

4 Ivo and Gratian, for the misfortune of Europe, received this into their codes (c. 15, qu. 6. 4).

5 Thus Anselm and Card. Gregory, and then Gratian, c. 11, qu. 8, 27,

If we look at the whole Papal system of universal monarchy, as it has been gradually built up during seven centuries, and is now being energetically pushed on to its final completion, we can clearly distinguish the separate stones the building is composed of. For a long time all that was done was to interpret the canon of Sardica so as to extend the appellant jurisdiction of the Pope to whatever could be brought under the general and elastic term of "greater causes." But from the end of the fifth century the Papal pretensions had advanced to a point beyond this, in consequence of the attitude assumed by Leo and Gelasius, and from that time began a course of systematic fabrications, sometimes manufactured in Rome, sometimes originating elsewhere, but adopted and utilized there.

The conduct of the Popes since Innocent I. and Zosimus, in constantly quoting the Sardican canon on appeals as a canon of Nice, cannot be exactly ascribed to conscious fraud — the arrangement of their collection of canons misled them. There was more deliberate purpose in inserting in the Roman manuscript of the sixth Nicene canon, "The Roman Church always had the primacy," of which there is no syllable in the original, — a fraud exposed at the Council of Chalcedon, to the confusion of the Roman legates, by reading the original.[1]

Towards the end of the fifth and beginning of the sixth century, the process of forgeries and fictions in the interests of Rome was actively carried on there. Then began the compilation of spurious acts of Roman martyrs, which was continued for some centuries, and which modern criticism, even at Rome, has been obliged to give up, as, for instance, is done by Papebroch, Ruinart, Orsi, and Saccarelli. *The fabulous story of the conversion and baptism of Constantine was invented to glorify the Church of Rome, and make Pope Silvester appear a worker of miracles.* Then the inviolability of the Pope had to be established, and the principle that he cannot be judged by any human tribunal, but only by himself. For four years before 514 Rome was the scene of a bloody strife about this question; the adherents of Symmachus and his opponent Laurentius murdered one another in the streets, and the Arian Goth, King Theodoric, was as little acceptable as a judge as the Emperor, who was hated in Rome. So the acts of the Council of Sinuessa and the legend of Pope Marcellinus were invented, and the "Constitution of Silvester," viz., the de-

---

[1] Mansi, *Concil.* vii. 444.

cision of a Synod of 284 bishops, pretended to have been held by him in 321 at Rome, evidently compiled while the bloody scenes in which clerics were murdered or executed for their crimes were fresh in men's minds. There again the principle was inculcated that no one can judge the first See.[1]

Some other records were fabricated at Rome in the same barbarous Latin, such as the *Gesta Liberii,* designed to confirm the legend of Constantine's baptism at Rome, and to represent Pope Liberius as purified from his heresy by repentance, and graced by a divine miracle. Of the same stamp were the *Gesta* of Pope Xystus III. and the History of Polychronius, where the Pope is accused, but the condemnation of his accuser follows, as also of the accuser of the fabulous Polychronius, Bishop of Jerusalem. These fabrications of the beginning of the sixth century, which all belong to the same class, had a reference also to the attitude of Rome towards the Church of Constantinople. It was the period of the long interruption of communion between East and West caused by the *Henoticon* (484-519), when Felix II. even summoned the Patriarch Acacius to Rome, and Pope Gelasius, about 495, for the first time insulted the Greeks and their twenty-eighth canon of Chalcedon, by affirming that every Council must be confirmed and every Church judged by Rome, but she can be judged by none. It was not by canons, as the Council of Chalcedon affirmed, but by the word of Chriist, that she received the primacy.[2] In this he went beyond all the claims of his predecessors. Thence came the fictions manufactured at Rome after his death, — a letter of the Nicene Council praying Pope Silvester for its confirmation, and the confirmation given by Silvester and a Roman Synod; the declaration in the acts of Xystus III. that the Emperor had convoked the Council by the Pope's authority; the History of Polychronius, exhibiting the Pope, as early as 435, sitting in judgment on an Eastern Patriarch; and lastly, the fabulous history of the Synod held by Silverster, which adopted Gelasius's saying about the divine origin of the Roman primacy, and confirmed the order of precedence of the Churches of Alexandria and Antioch next after Rome, making no mention of Constantinople, and thus upsetting the canons of 381 and 451, which gave her the precedence.[3]

---

1 *Append. ad Epp. Pont. Rom.* (ed. Coustant), pp. 38 *seq.*

2 Mansi, viii. 54.

3 These documents are printed from mss. of the eighth century in Amort's *Elementa Juris Canon.* ii. 432-486.

While this tendency to forging documents was so strong in Rome, it is remarkable that for a thousand years no attempt was made there to form a collection of canons of her own, such as the Easterns had as early as the fifth century, clearly because for a long time Rome took so very little part in ecclesiastical legislation. No doubt constant appeal was made to the canons of Councils, and Rome professed her resolve to secure their observance with all her might, and by her conspicuous example; but the canon she had chiefly at heart was the third of Sardica, and the Sardican canons were never received at all in the East.[1] When Dionysius gave the Roman Church her first tolerably comprehensive collection of canons, viz., his translation of the Greek canons, with the African and Sardican, more than twenty Synods had been held in Rome since 313, but there were no records of them to be found.

Towards the end of the sixth century a fabrication was undertaken in Rome, the full effect of which did not appear till long afterwards. The famous passage in St. Cyprian's book on the Unity of the Church was adorned, in Pope Pelagius II.'s letter to the Istrian bishops, with such additions as the Roman pretensions required. St. Cyprian said that all the Apostles had received from Christ equal power and authority with Peter, and this was too glaring a contradiction of the theory set up since the time of Gelasius. So the following words were interpolated: "The primacy was given to Peter to show the unity of the Church and of the chair. How can he believe himself to be in the Church who forsakes the chair of Peter, on which the Church is built?"[2] The varying judgments of the later Roman clergy on Cyprian, who had up to his death been a decided opponent of Rome, seem to have had an influence on this interpolation. He was at first almost the only foreign martyr whose annual feast was kept in Rome; but after Gelasius had included his writings in a list of works rejected by the Church, it became necessary to find some way of reconciling the high reverence accorded to the man with the disapproval of his writings. This seems to have led to the interpolation, so that the first rank among orthodox Fathers was assigned to Cyprian in the revised edition of the catalogue of Gelasius, in direct contradiction to the passage in the same decree

---

1 Dionysius Exiguus observes this in the Preface to the second edition of his Collection, prepared by command of Pope Hormisdas. See Andres, *Lettera a G. Morelli* (Parma, 1802), p. 66. It will be seen that there was always a quarrel about the Nicene canons, and one party wished to replace them probably the sixth canon) by others. This points to the decisions of Silvester and his Synod, mentioned above.
2 Cf. the notes of Rigualt, Baluze, and Krabinger, to their editions of Cyprian.

placing him among "apocryphal," viz., rejected authors.[1] But as Cyprian's writings had not spread from Rome, but had long been much read in the Gallican and North Italian Churches, the additions did not get into the manuscripts.

Earlier than this an interpolation of the old catalogue of Roman bishops had been undertaken for a definite purpose, and thus the foundation was laid of the *Liber Pontificalis,*[2] afterwards enlarged. It exists in Schelstrate's edition, in its original from, of about 530.[3] The second edition, and continuation to the time of Conon (687) written about 730, and afterwards brought down to 724 by the same hand, is based on contemporary records for the sixth and seventh century. It is the first edition of 530 which is chiefly to be reckoned as a calculated forgery, and an important link in the chain of Roman inventions and interpolations. It is all composed in the barbarous and ungrammatical Latin common to the Roman fabrications of the sixth century.[4] The objects were — *first,* to attest the mass of spurious acts of Roman martyrs, and the reiterated statements that the earliest Popes had appointed a number of notaries to compile these acts, and seven deacons to superintend them; *secondly,* to confirm the existing legends of Popes and Emperors, — such as the Roman baptism of Constantine, the stories about Silvester, Felix, and Liberius, Xystus III., and the like; *thirdly,* to assign a greater antiquity to some later liturgical usages; *fourthly,* to exhibit the Popes as legislators for the whole Church, although, apart from the liturgical directions ascribed to them, and the constantly recurring assertion that they had marked out the parishes and the hierarchial grades of the clergy in Rome, no particular ordinances of theirs could be quoted, and people had to be content with stating generally that Damasus

---

1 When in later times Cyprian was edited at Rome by Manutius in 1563, the Roman censors insisted on the interpolated passages being retained, though not found in the MSS., as the editor, Latino Latini, complains in his Letters (Viterbii, 1667, ii. 109). The minister, Cardinal Fleury, made the came conditions for the Paris edition of Baluze. See Chiniac, *Histoire des Capitul.* (Paris, 1772), p. 226. The minister named a commission to decide whether the interpolations erased by Baluze, and expunged from every critical edition, should be printed, but Fleury was Cardinal as well as minister, and "a moins que de vouloir se faire une querelle d'etat avec Rome imperieuse, il falloit que le passage fut restitue, parceque en le laissant supprime en vertu d'une decision ministerielle, il auroit semble qu'on vouloit porter atteinte a la primaute Romaine. Le passage fut restitue par le moyen d'un carton."

2 The *Liber Pontificalis,* or *Anastasius* (falsely so called), was usually quoted as a work of Pope Damasus in the middle ages.

3 He has collated the two editions in his *Antiq. Eccl. Rom.* 1963, i. 402-495; in parallel columns.

4 See the careful analysis of the whole work in Piper's *Einleitung in die Monum. Theol.* (Gotha, 1867), pp. 315-349.

or Gelasius or Hilary had made a law binding the whole Church.[1]
In the later and more historical portion (from 440 to 530) the
Pope is specially represented as teacher of doctrine and supreme
judge, with a view to the Greeks. In the first edition every historical
notice, except about buildings, sacred offerings, and cemeteries,
is false; the author's statements about the fortunes and acts of
particular Popes never agree with what is known of their history,
but rather contradict it, sometimes glaringly; and thus we must
regard as fabulous even what cannot be proved such from
sources now accessible to us, for there is almost always an obvious
design.[2]

The fictions of the *Liber Pontificalis* had a far-reaching influence after they became known, and were used — first by Bede
about 710 — in the rest of the West. They supplied the basis
for the notion of the Popes having constantly acted from the first
as legislators of the whole Church, and they greatly helped on the
later fabrication of Isidore, who incorporated these records of
Papal enactments into his decretals, and thereby gave them an appearance of being genuine. This agreement of the forged decretals
with the annals of the Popes is what gave the former so long a hold
on public belief.

*After the middle of the eighth century, the famous Donation of
Constantine was concocted at Rome. It is based on the earlier
fifth-century legend of his cure from leprosy, and baptism by
Pope Silvester, which is repeated at length, and the Emperor is
said, out of gratitude, to have bestowed Italy and the western
provinces on the Pope, and also to have made many regulations
about the honorary prerogatives and dress of the Roman clergy.[3]
The Pope is, moreover, represented as lord and master of all
bishops, and having authority over the four great thrones of
Antioch, Alexandria, Constantinople, and Jerusalem.*

---

1 The phrase "fecit Constitutum de omni Ecclesia" is repeated on nearly every page,
but what the ordinance was is never specified, while the pretended liturgical ap-
pointments are always precisely expressed.

2 The *Liber Pontificalis* has been critically examined by Tillemont, and more fully by
Coustant, and its gross anachronisms proved, so that there can be no doubt about
its fabulous character, and it gives one the impression throughout of deliberate
fraud. Clearly the compilers had no historical or documentary evidence. The first
enlargement of the Liberian catalogue reached almost to Damasus, and must have
been composed early in the sixth century. The two letters of Damasus and Jerome
were invented for it, according to which Damasus collected and sent to St. Jerome
what could be found of the biographies of the Popes. In a second and altered
edition, some twenty years later, about 536, was added to the list of Popes from
Damasus to Felix IV. This last part, from 440, historical, but strongly coloured,
and garnished with fables devised in the interest of Rome.

3 The "western provinces" must not be understood of Gaul, Spain, etc. The phrase
is used for the northern parts of the Peninsula—Lombardy, Venetia, and Istria,—
which do not properly belong to Roman Italy.

The forgery betrayed its Roman authorship in every line; it is self-evident that a cleric of the Lateran Church was the composer. The document was obviously intended to be shown to the Frankish king, Pepin, and must have been compiled just before 754. Constantine relates in it how he served the Pope as his groom, and led his horse some distance. This induced Pepin to offer the Pope a homage, so foreign to Frankish ideas, and the Pope told him from the first that he expected, not a gift, but restitution from him and his Franks.[1] The first reference to this gift of Constantine occurs in Hadrian's letter to Charles the Great in 777, where he tells him that, as the new Constantine, he has indeed given the Church what is her own, but that he has more of the old Imperial endowments to restore to her. The Popes had already been accustomed, for several years, since 752, to speak, not of gifts, but restitutions, in their letters; the Italian towns and provinces were to be restored, sometimes to St. Peter, sometimes to the Roman republic.[2] Such language first became intelligible when the Donation of Contantine was brought forward to show that the Pope was the rightful possessor as heir of the Roman Caesars in Italy; for, he being at once the successor of Peter and of Constantine, what was given to the Roman Republic was given to Peter and *vice versa*. In this way it was made clear to Pepin that he had simply to reject the demands of the Greek Imperial Court about the restoration of its territory as unauthorized.

It would indeed be incomprehensible how Pepin could have been induced to give the Exarchate, with twenty towns, to the Pope, who never possessed it, and thereby to draw on himself the enmity of the still powerful Imperial Court, merely that

---

1 There can be no doubt as to the Roman origin of the "Donation." The Jesuit Cantel has rightly recognised this in his *Hist. Metrop. Urb.* p. 195. He thinks a Roman subdeacon, John, was the author. The document had a threefold object,—against the Longobards, who were threatening Rome, against the Greeks, who would acknowledge no supremacy of the Roman See over their Church, and with a view to the Franks. The attempt of the Jesuits in the *Civilta* to make a Frank the author, simply because Aeneas of Pairs and Ado of Vienne mention the gift in the ninth century, is not worth serious notice; it refutes itself. There is the closest agreement in style and idea between the "Donation" and contemporary Roman documents, especially the *Constitutum Pauli I.* (Harduin, *Concil.* iii. 1999 *seq.*) and the *Epistola S. Petri*, compiled in 753 or 754. The Phrase "Concinnatio luminarium," used only in Papal letters of that date, and in the *Constitutum* and *Donatio*, betrays a Roman hand. So does the form of imprecation and threat of hell-torments, found in the *Constitutum* and *Epistola S. Petri*, and the term "Satrapae," wholly foreign to the West, and found only in the "Donation," and in contemporary Papal letters. See Cenni, *Monum. Dominat. Pontif.* i. 154.

2 "Exarchatum Ravenae et rei-publicae jura seu loca *reddere*" is the phrase in the *Liber Pontif.* See Le Cointe, *Annal. Eccl. Franc.* v. 424. Again, in the letter of Pope Stephen we read, "per Donationis paginam civitates et loca . . . *restituenda* confirmastis." And so constantly when the Exarchate and Pentapolis are spoken of.

the lamps in the Roman churches might be furnished with oil,[1] had he not been shown that the Pope had a right to it by the gift of Constantine, and terrified by the threat of vengeance from the Prince of the Apostles, if his property should be withheld. There was no fear of such documents as the Epistle of Peter and the Donation of Constantine being critically examined at the warlike Court of Pepin. Men who might be written to that their bodies and souls would be eternally lacerated and tormented in hell if they did not fight against the enemies of the Church, believed readily enough that Constantine had given Italy to Pope Silvester. Those were days of darkness in France, and, in the complete extinction of all learning, there was not a single man about Pepin whose sharpsightedness the Roman agents had reason to dread.[2]

One is tempted to ascribe to the same hand the Epistle of St. Peter to his "adopted son" the King of the Franks, which appeared also at this moment of great danger and distress, as well as of lofty hopes and pretensions, — a fabrication which for strangeness and audacity has never been exceeded. Entreating and promising victory, and then again threatening the pains of hell, the Prince of the Apostles adjures the Franks to deliver Rome and the Roman Church. The Epistle really went from Rome to the Frankish kingdom, and seems to have produced its effect there.[3]

Twenty years later the need was felt at Rome of a more extensive invention or interpolation. Pepin had given the Pope the Exarchate, taken away from the Longobards, with Ravenna for its capital, and twenty other towns of the Emilia, Flaminia, and Pentapolis, or the triangle of coast between Bologna, Comacchio, and Ancona.[4] More he had been unable to give, for this was all the territory the Longobards had shortly before acquired, and were now obliged to give up. In 774 Pepin's son, Charles the Great, after taking Pavia, became king of the Longobardic territory, stretching far southwards. No more could be said about the gift of Constantine; Charles would have had at once to abdicate. Moreover, a strong Italian soverign was wanted at Rome, who from his own part of the peninsula could also keep the Papal dominions

---

1 This was always given in the covetous begging-letters of the Popes as their main ground for demanding the gifts of land they wished for.

2 See the Benedictine *Hist. Lit. de la France*, iv. 8.

3 It was incorporated in the official collection of the *Codex Carolinus*. Cf. Cenni, *op. cit.* 150.

4 This is clear from the enumerations in the *Liber Pontif.* and the notice in Leo of Ostia. See Le Cointe, v. 484, and Mock, *De Donat a Car. M. oblata*, pp. 8 *seq.*

in subjection; at the same time, the Roman lust for land and subjects and revenues was not long satisfied with the Exarchate and its belongings. So a document was laid before the King in Rome, professing to be his father's gift or promise *(promissio)* of Kiersy. He renewed it, as it was shown him, and gave away thereby the greater part of Italy, including a good deal that did not belong to him; for the document, as quoted in Adrian's Biography, specifies as territories to be assigned to the Popes all Corsica, Venetia, and Istria, Luni, Monselice, Parma, Reggio, Mantva, the duchies of Spoleto and Benevento, and the Exarchate.[1]

It has seemed to every one mysterious and inexplicable that Charlemagne should have made so comprehensive a gift, leaving himself but little of his Italian kingdom. Accordingly Muratori, Sugenheim, Hegel, Gregorovius, and Niehues have either declared the passage spurious, or accused the Papal biographer of falsehood; else, observes Niehues, we must accuse Charles of consciously indorsing a perjury, and Adrian of a cowardly negligence.[2] Abel thinks the suspicions against the genuineness of the passage are strong, but not conclusive, and contents himself with assuming that the gift was really equal to Pepin's, but was very limited.[3] Lastly, Mock accepts the extent of the gift, but rejects its equality to Pepin's, and therefore the truth of Adrian's Biography; and Baxmann, the latest authority, leaves all uncertain.[4] In short, no one has succeeded in unravelling the secret.

But the thing explains itself when we compare the twice printed and wholly fabulous document,[5] professing to be the pact or bond of Pepin, and which really describes the geographical extent of the gift as it is stated in Adrian's Biography, only with the addition of more names of towns. This document is closely related to the Donation of Constantine. Like Constantine, Pepin gives an express account of his relations to the Pope as an explanation to the Greeks and Lombards of his gifts, and disclaims for himself and his successors all interest in the alienated territories, except the right of having prayers offered for the rest of their souls, and the title of a Roman patrician; for those territories were become the lawful property of the Pope through so many imperial deeds

---

1 *Lib. Pontif.* (ed Vignol.) ii. 193.

2 *Geschichte des Verhaltn. zwischen Kaiserthum und Pabsthum.* 1. 565.

3 *Forschungen zur deutchen Geschichte,* i. 469 *seq. Jahrbuch,* i. 181.

4 *Politik der Pabste.* 1. 277.

5 Fantuzzi, *Monum. Ravennati.* vi. 264; Troya, *Codice diplom. Longobard.* (Napoli, 1854), iv. 503 *seq.* Troya thinks the document genuine, which is unintelligible in a man of his information.

of gift. For this document, obviously composed in the style of the Donation of Constantine and the Roman biographies of Popes, it is difficult to assign any other origin or object than the purpose of having it laid before Charlemagne;[1] and it shows how he was induced to make a promise he found it impossible to keep; for he henceforth vigorously withstood the perpetually renewed demands of the Popes, and made the counter requisition that Rome should prove its title to each particular domain separately.

There have unquestionably been some falsifications in the privileges granted to the Roman See by Emperors later than Charles the Great, though they do not go so far as has often been maintained. The pact or gift of Louis the Pious in 817 bears internal signs of genuineness, but has evidently been interpolated.[2] It makes the Emperor give the islands of Corsica, Sardinia, and Sicily, with the opposite coasts, and all Tuscany and Spoleto, to Pope Pascal. It is needless to observe that if Louis had really partly given and partly confirmed to the Pope the greater part of Italy in this elastic and unlimited fashion, the whole subsequent history of the Papacy to Gregory VII. would be an insoluble riddle; for the Popes neither possessed nor once claimed those territories, which together make up a large kingdom. Innocent III. was the first to maintain that all Tuscany belonged to the Popes; no one did so before him. Gregory VII. first claimed the duchy of Spoleto. The falsification certainly took place towards the end of the eleventh century, when matters were managed so actively and astutely at Rome; for Gregory VII. was also the first to claim Sardinia, but he takes occasion to observe that the Sardinians have hitherto had no relations with the Roman See, or rather, as he thinks, have become as much strangers to it, through the negligence of his predecessors, as the people at the ends of the earth.[3] Urban II., indeed, in 1091, proved that Corsica was a Papal fief, not merely from the gift of Louis or Charlemagne, but from the Donation of Constantine, which, as then interpreted, assigned to Pope Silvester all islands of the West, includ-

---

1 It must else have been meant for the eye of one of the later Carlovingians. Clearly it was designed for the eye of a Frankish king, and after the establishment of the empire Pepin's disclaimer of reserving any power in the alienated dominions would have no further object. We must therefore hold to Charles the Great, and the date of 774, and attribute the wrong name of the Pope to the ignorance of a later copyist.

2 It has been held as a pure invention by most scholars, as Pagi, Muratori, Beretto, Le Bret, Pertz, Gregorovius, Baxmann, and lastly, that great master in the criticism of the Caroline documents, Sickel, while Marini (*Nuovo Esame*, etc., Roma, 1822) and Gfrorer defend it as genuine.

3 *Epist.* i. 29.

ing the Balearic Isles, and *even Ireland*. So again with the privileges of the Emperors Otho I. in 962, and Henry II. in 1020. The documents are in both cases genuine, or copies of genuine ones, in the main, but the statement of the *Liber Pontificalis* about Charlemagne's Donation was manifestly interpolated wholesale afterwards.[1]

It is well known that the Countess Matilda, who was entirely under the influence of Gregory VII. and Anselm of Lucca, gave Liguria and Tuscany to the Roman See in 1077.[2] When we remember that Gregory VII., in 1081, required of the pretender Rudolph an oath that he would restore the lands and revenues which Constantine and Charlemagne had given to St. Peter,[3] that Leo IX. had already solemnly appealed to the Donation of Constantine, and that Matilda's adviser, Anselm, had inserted this Donation in his Codex, we may easily judge what document was used to convince her that she was obligated in conscience to make so extensive an abdication or restitution.

We cannot suppose that such a man as Gregory VII. would consciously take part in these fabrications, but, in his unlimited credulity and eager desire for territory and dominion, he appealed to the first forged document that came to hand as a solid proof. Thus, in 1081, he affirmed that, according to the documents preserved in the archives of St. Peter's, Charles the Great had made the whole of Gaul tributary to the Roman Church, and given to her all Saxony.[4] A document forged at Rome in the tenth or eleventh century is undoubtedly referred to, which may be found in Torrigio.[5] Charles there calls himself Emperor in the year 797, and his kingdoms are Francia, Aquitania, and Gaul; Alcuin is his Chancellor, and each of his kingdoms is to pay an annual tribute of 400 pounds to Rome.

We have put forward these facts about the deeds of gift, because they set in a clear light the line habitually followed at Rome from the sixth to the twelfth century, and because their authors

---

1 Cf. Watterich, *Vitae Pont.* i. 45; Hefele, *Concil. Geschichte*, iv. 580; *Beitrage*, i. 255.

2 Leo Cassinensis in Pertz, *Monum. Germ.* ix. 738. Liguria means the Lombardic duchies belonging to Matilda.

3 *Ep.* viii. 8. 26.

4 *Ep.* viii, 23.

5 *Le Grotte Vaticane* (Roma, 1639), pp. 505-510. As Acts of the Martyrs had been fabricated there earlier, so, from the tenth century, false documents were fabricated wholesale at Rome, as the monographs about particular Roman churches prove. So the first document of 570 Marini quotes (*Papiri Diplom.*, Roma, 1805) is an invention. See Jaffe, *Regesta*, p. 936.

are undoubtedly the very persons chargeable with the fictions undertaken in the interests of ecclesiastical supremacy. We shall now continue our enumeration and examination of the forgeries by which the whole constitution of the Church was gradually changed.

The pseudo-Isidorian forgery of the middle of the ninth century has been already mentioned. Rome, as we have seen, had no part in that, though she afterwards took full advantage of it for extending her power, the substance of these forgeries being incorporated into the canonical collections of the Gregorian party.

The most potent instrument of the new Papal system was Gratian's *Decretum*, which issued about the middle of the twelfth century from the first school of Law in Europe, the juristic teacher of the whole of Western Christendom, Bologna. In this work the Isidorian forgeries were combined with those of the Gregorian writers, Deusdedit, Anselm, Gregory of Pavia, and with Gratian's own additions. His work displaced all the older collections of canon law, and became the manual and repertory, not for canonists only, but for the scholastic theologians, who, for the most part, derived all their knowledge of Fathers and Councils from it. No book has ever come near it in its influence in the Church, although there is scarcely another so chokefull of gross errors, both intentional and unintentional. Not only Anselm, Deusdedit, and Cardinal Gregory, whose works had little circulation, but also the German Burkard (or his assistant, the Abbot Olbert) had pioneered the way for Gratian. Burkard had not only made copious use of the Isidorian fictions in his Collection, compiled between 1012 and 1024, but had also ascribed the ecclesiastical decisions in the capitularies to various Popes, so that from the middle of the eleventh century the erroneous notion took rise that the free determinations of Frankish Synods in the ninth century were the autocratic commands of Popes. All these fabrications — the rich harvest of three centuries — Gratian inserted in good faith into his collection, but he also added, knowingly and deliberately, a number of fresh corruptions, all in the spirit and interest of the Papal system.

It may be shown by certain examples, going deep into the development of the new Church system, how Gratian the Italian forwarded by his own interpolations the grand national scheme of making the whole Christian world, in a certain sense, the domain of the Italian clergy, through the Papacy. The German and West Frankish bishops had already bowed to the Isidorian decretals.

Their influence is shown in the decisions of the German National Synod at Tribur in 895. We may see here how deeply the pseudo-Isidore, with the imperial dignity of his Popes, and their dictatorial commands, had penetrated into the very lifeblood of the German hierarchy. It came to this, that the bishops had bound themselves most closely to King Arnulf, who was present, and took a prominent part in the Synod, and that he, desiring the imperial crown, which had already once allured him into Italy, could only obtain it by the favour of Pope Formosus. So they decided that, though the yoke of Rome should become intolerable, it ought to be borne with pious resignation.

How often has this saying been repeated since! It was ascribed to Charles the Great, just as Constantine is affirmed to have called the Pope a God. And since Gratian adopted it as a capitulary of Charles, and stamped it as a universal canon,[1] it became the current view up to the time of the Council of Constance, albeit sometimes contradicted in act, that it is a duty to endure the unendurable if Rome imposes it.

The corruption of the thirty-sixth canon of the OEcumenical Council of 692 is Gratian's own doing.[2] It renewed the canon of Chalcedon (451), which gave the Patriarch of New Rome, or Constantinople, equal rights with the Roman Patriarch. Gratian, by a change of two words, gives it a precisely opposite sense, and suppresses the reference to the canon of Chalcedon. He also reduces the five Patriarchs to four; for the ancient equality of position of the Roman bishop and the four chief bishops of the East was now to disappear, though even the Gregorians, as, *e.g.,* Anselm, had treated him as one of the Patriarchs.[3] There was no longer any room for the patriarchal dignity of the Roman See; he who had drawn to himself every conceivable right in the Church could hardly exercise a particular patriarchal power in one portion of it. The plenary powers of the Pope were become a *mare magnum,* within which there could be no sea or lake of special privileges.[4] This showed itself conspicuously in reference to the provinces of Eastern Illyricum, — Macedonia, Thessaly, Epirus,

---

1 Dist. 19, c. 3.

2 *Dist.* 22. 6. The Roman correctors have substituted "nec non" for Gratian's fabrication of "non tamen," which was left for 400 years.

3 Anselm and Deusdedit set aside the famous decree of Nicolas II, giving the German Emperor the right of confirming Papal elections, on the ground that one patriarch, the Roman, could not annul the decision of five patriarchs at Constantinople.

4 The numberless privileges accorded by Popes to the Mendicant Orders were afterwards called a "Mare magnum."

Dardania, — which were before under the patriarchal jurisdiction of the Roman bishop, so that the metropolian of Thessalonica was appointed his vicar over them. The Emperor Leo, the Isaurian, separated those provinces from Rome about 730, and they now belonged to the patriarchate of Constantinople. There was a long dispute about it; the perpetually renewed demands of the Popes gained no attention at Constantinople till the establishment of the Latin Empire there in 1204 gave them power for the moment in these Eastern lands also. And it is significant that Innocent III., far from attmpting to resume his ancient patriarchal rights there, made the Bishop of Tornobus Patriarch, — an ephemeral creation, soon to be again extinguished.[1]

The canon of the African Synod, — that immoveable stumbling-block of all Papalists, — which forbids any appeal beyond the seas, *i.e.*, to Rome, Gratian adapted to the service of the new system by an addition which made the Synod affirm precisely what it denies. If Isidore undertook by his fabrications to annul the old law forbidding bishops being moved from one see to another, Gratian, following Anselm and Cardinal Gregory, improved on this by a fresh forgery, appropriating to the Pope alone the right of translation.[2] One of the most important of his additions, and also an evidence of the wide divergence between the old and new Church law, is the chapter — also based on Anselm, Deusdedit, and Cardinal Gregory — which elaborated a system of religious persecution.[3] While, on the one hand, by falsifying a canon quoted by Ivo and Burkard, he makes Gregory the Great order that the Church should protect homicides and murderers;[4] on the other hand, he takes great pains to inculcate, in a long series of canons, that it is lawful, nay, a duty, to constrain men to goodness, and therefore to faith, and to what was then reckoned matter of faith, by all means of physical compulsion, and particularly to torture and execute heretics, and confiscate their property. In this he went beyond the Gregorian canonists. He does not fail to urge that Urban II. had declared any one who should kill an excommunicated person, out of zeal to the Church, to be by no means a murderer, and hence draws the general conclusion that it is clear the "bad" — all who are declared "bad" by the Church authorities — are not only to be scourged, but executed.

---

1 Quien, *Oriens Christ.* i. 96-98; ii. 24, 25.
2 *Caus.* 7. Q. i. 84.
3 *Caus.* 23, Q. iv. 4, 5.
4 *Caus.* 23, Q. v. 7.

Still worse things may be found in the work of the Bolognese monk, which, through the instrumentality of the *Curia,* became the manual and canonical code of the West, to the scandal of religion and the Church, and this medley, not of simple, but complicated and multiplied forgeries, was rich in materials containing the germ of future developments, and cutting deep in their consequences into both the civil and ecclesiastical life of the West. So was it with the idea of heresy, which even then was fashioned into a two-edged sword, and veritable instrument of ecclesiastical domination. Pope Nicolas I. had affirmed, in his letter to the Greek Emperor Michael, that by the sixth canon of the Œcumenical Council of 381 (the first of Constantinople), which he grossly distorted, schismatics and excommunicated men were to be treated as heretics. Anselm and Gratian embodied this statement in their new codes;[1] so that at the very time when heresy was stamped as a capital offence, the term received a terrible and unlimited extension, as indeed everything had been done by earlier fabrications to make heretics of all who dared to disobey a Papal command, or speak against a Papal decision on doctrine.

The earlier Gregorians had not laid down so clearly and nakedly as Gratian, that in his unlimited superiority to all law, the Pope stands on an equality with the Son of God. *Gratian says that, as Christ submitted to the law on earth, though in truth he was its Lord, so the Pope is high above all laws of the Church, and can dispose of them as he will, since they derive all their force from him alone.*[2] This became, and chiefly through Gratian's influence, the prevalent doctrine of the *Curia,* so that even after the great reforming Councils, Eugenius IV., in 1439, answered King Charles VII., when he appealed to the laws of the Church, that it was simply ludicrous to come with such an appeal to the Pope, who remits, suspends, changes, or annuls these laws at his good pleasure.[3]

In the fifty years between the appearance of Gratian's *Decretum* and the pontificate of the most powerful of the Popes, Innocent III., the Papal system, such as it had become in its three stages of development, through the pseudo-Isidore, the Gregorian school, and Gratian, worked its way to complete dominion. In the Roman courts Gratian's Code was acted upon — at Bologna it was taught; even the Emperor Frederick I. had his son Henry VI. instructed

---

1 *Caus.* 4. Q. i. c. 2.

2 *Caus,* 25, Q. i. c. 11, 12, 16.

3 Raynald, anno 1439, 37.

in the *Decretum* and Roman law.[1] The whole decretal legislation from 1159 to 1320 is built upon the foundation of Gratian. The same is true of Aquinas's dogmatic theology on all kindred points, as, indeed, the whole scholastic system in questions of Church constitution was modelled on the favourite science of the clergy of the period, Jurisprudence, as interpreted by Gratian, Raymund, and other compilers of decretals. The theologians borrowed theory, texts, and proofs, alike from these compilations. As early as the twelfth century, in quoting a passage from Gratian, the Popes used to say, it was *"in sacris canonibus,"* or *"in. decretis."*[2] And about 1570, the Roman correctors of the *Decretum,* appointed by three Popes, said the work was intrusted to them, that the authority of this most useful and weighty Codex might not be weakened.[3] So high stood the character of this work, saturated through and through as it is with deceit and error and forgeries, which, like a great wedge driven into the fabric of the Church, gradually loosened, disjointed, and disintegrated the whole of its ancient order, not, indeed, without putting another, and, in its way, very strong constitution in its place.

§ VIII. *Progress of the Papal Power*

Alexander III. (1159-81) and Innocent III. (1198-1216) were the chief authors of the development of the new system, and creators of the decretal canon law, through the number of edicts, and the unity and coherence of their policy, based on one fundamental idea. The notion is more prominent with Innocent then even with Gregory VII., that the Pope is God's *locum tenens* on earth, set to watch over the social, political, and religious condition of mankind, like a Divine Providence, as chief overseer and lord, who must put down all opposition. The radical principle with him, as with Gregory, is that all rank and authority not held by priests is an incongruity in the Divine plan of the world, introduced through human folly and sinfulness, while the priesthood is, properly speaking, the sole ordinance and institution of God.[4] Gregory had declared, of course in direct contradiction to the Gospel teaching about the Divine institition of government, that

---

1 Cf. Bohmer, *Diss. de decr. Grat.* in Pref. to his *Corp. Jur. Can.* p. xvii.

2 Thus Alex. III. (*Decr. c. 6 de Despons. unpub.*), Clem. III. (*De Jure Patron,* c. 25), and Innoc. iii., cite Gratian with the words, "in corpore decretorum."

3 "Ne hujusce utilissimi et gravissimi Codicis vacillaret auctoritas."

4 See *Ep. ad Joan, Angl. Reg.* in Rymer's *Foedera Reg. Angl.* i, 1, 119, "Institutum fuit sacerdotium per ordinationem Divinam, Aegnum autem per extortionem humanam," etc.

the royal power was set up at the instigation of Satan, by persons ignorant of God, and full of crimes, out of mere lust of dominion, whereas before men had been equal.[1]

New means of influence accrued to the Roman See through the Crusades, and the consequent change in the system of penance and indulgences, the privileges awarded to Crusaders, and the leadership in these holy wars, which, as a matter of course, devolved on the Popes. The same end was served by the *military Orders,* which acknowledged the Pope as their only superior; the constant union with France, clergy as well as kings (before 1300); and still more by the intellectual power the Papal monarchy derived from the two great Universities — Bologna, the school of Papal canon law, and Paris, the home of scholasticism, which was more and more lending itself to the Papal system. But, above all, from the beginning of the thirteenth century, the new Religious Orders of Mendicants, which swarmed over the whole Christian world — Franciscans, Dominicans, Augustinians, and Carmelites, especially the two first — *were the strongest pillars and supports* of this monarchy. After the Isidorian decretals and Gratian, the introduction of these Orders, with their rigid monarchical organization, was the third great lever whereby the old Church system, resting on the gradation of bishops, presbyteries, and parish priests, was undermined and destroyed. Completely under the Roman control, and acting everywhere as Papal delegates, wholly independent of bishops, with plenary power to encroach on the rights of parish priests, these monks set up their own churches in the Church, laboured for the honour and greatness of their Order, and for the Papal authority on which their prerogatives rested. We may say that that authority was literally doubled through their means. They became masters of literature, of the pulpits, and of the university chairs; they travelled about as Papal tax-gatherers and preachers of indulgences, with plenary power, even of inflicting excommunication. And thus the spiritual campaign organized at Rome was carried into every village, and the *parish clergy generally succumbed to the mendicants, armed as they were with privileges from head to heel.* For they possessed and used the effective expedients of *easy absolution, and new devotions and methods of salvation, invented by themselves,* to which the parish priests had nothing to oppose, while their isolation made

---

1 *Epist.* lib. viii. Ep 21: "Quis nesciat, reges et duces ab iis habuisse principium, qui Deum ignorantes, superbia, rapinis, perfidii, homicidiis postremo universis pene sceleribus, mundai principe diabolo videlicet agitante, dominari caeca cupiditate et intolerabili praesumtione affectaverunt!"

every attempt at open resistance on their part useless. They could compel both priest and people, by excommunication, to hear them preach the Papal indulgences, and could absolve from reserved sins in the confessional. Bishops and priests felt their impotence against the new power of these monks, strengthened by the Inquisition, and had, however indignantly, to bend under the yoke laid on their necks by two powers irresistible in their union.

If Gregory VIII. supported his new claims, his political lordship and subjugation of the monarchy, on falsehoods, not indeed of his own coining, Innocent III. went further in this direction, and dealt with history as with the Bible, according to the exigencies of the case. He invented the story that the Empire had been transferred from the Greeks to the Franks by a Papal sentence;[1] and thence inferred that the German princes derived their right of electing the Emperor from the Pope only, and asserted that he had the right of rejecting their nominee. Later Papal authors have transformed these assertions into historical facts invented by themselves.

One of Gregory VII.'s maxims, ascribing personal holiness to every rightly elected Pope, was suffered to drop. There was danger of the want of holiness suggesting the invalidity of the election, and therefore the decretal books, while upholding the rest of Gregory's postulates, were silent about this. Moreover, everyone knew and said that simony, which was generally treated as heresy, was rampant in the Roman Court, and that taking bribes for benefices and legal proceedings was a daily occurrence with the Popes and Cardinals. The charge of heresy going on under the very eyes of the Pope, and with his express or tacit consent could not be answered, and was constantly urged, till the canonists hit upon the resource of maintaining that what was simony in others was not simony in the Pope, because he is superior to law, and everything in the Church is his property, which he can deal with as he will.[2]

The Gregorian system required the most complete immunity of the whole clergy from the secular power and civil courts. It served to create an immense army, exclusively belonging to the Pope, and widely separated by common caste feeling and caste interests from the lay world. Every clergyman was to recognise but one lord and ruler, the Pope, who disposed of him indirectly, through the bish-

---

1 *De Elect.* c. 34.

2 Thus the canonist John of God, about 1245, quotes and repudiates the statement, "Lex Julia dicit quod apud Roman simonia non committitur" (*De Poen. D. Papae*). See excerpts in *Theodori Poenitent.* (ed. Petit.) Paris, 1677. There was a long controversy about it.

ops, who were bound by oath to himself, or directly, in cases of exemption, and used him as a tool for the execution of his commands. Gratian has adapted his Codex to these views, partly by means of the pseudo-Isidorian fabrications, partly by later corruptions of his own and the Gregorians.[1] The Papal prescriptions in the code of decretals, completely establish the principle that clerics are exempt from secular courts, and that by Divine ordinance.[2] The Popes added that no cleric could renounce this privilege, as it belonged to the whole Church.

One would have supposed there would be no further need for so perilous an instrument as falsification of texts, when all that was required for the development of Papal domination in Church and State could easily be built on the strong and broad foundation of Gratian's *Decretum.* And yet the same method was still pursued, and that too with texts of Scripture. Innocent III. wished to make Deuteronomy a code for Christians, that he might get Bible authority for his doctrine of Papal power over life and death; but for that the words had to be altered. It is there said that an Israelite may appeal to the high priest and chief judge, and if he does not abide by their sentence shall be put to death.[3] Innocent, by a slight interpolation in the text of the Vulgate, made this into a statement that whoever does not submit to the decision of the high priest (whose place the Pope occupies under the New Covenant) is to be sentenced by the judge to execution.[4] And Leo X. quoted the passage with the same corruption, in a Bull of his, giving a false reference to the Book of Kings instead of Deuteronomy, to prove that whoever disobeyed the Pope must be put to death.[5]

Innocent went beyond Gratian, above all, in fixing the relations of the Church to the State and secular princes. He taught that the Papal power is to the imperial and royal as the sun to the moon, which last has only a borrowed light, or the soul to the body, which exists not for itself, but only to be the slave of the soul, and the two swords (Luke xxii. 38) are a symbol of the ecclesiastical and secular power, both of which belong to the Pope, but he wields one himself and intrusts the other to princes to use

---

1 Thus (*Caus.* ii. Q. i. c. 5) he has expunged the words of a law of Theodosius confining the exemption to spiritual matters, and thereby wholly altered it. So (*ib.* c. 5) he changed the words "sine scientia Pontificis" into "sine licentia," to make the civil authority over clerics dependent on delegation from the bishops.

2 *Decr. de Judic.* c. 4, 8, 10; *De Foro Compet.* c. i. 2. Q. 12, 13.

3 Deut. xvii. 12.

4 *Decr. Per Venerabilem,* "Qui filli sint legitimi," 4. 17.

5 *Pastor Aeternus, Harduin, Concil.* ix. 1826.

at his behest, and for the service of the Church.[1] In his famous decretal *Novit*, Innocent was the first to lay down the theory, often repeated by later Popes, that wherever a serious sin has been committed, or is charged by one party on the other, it behooves the Pope to interpose with his judgment, to punish, and to annul the decisions of the civil tribunal.[2] The principle this newly devised claim is based upon must apply to every clergyman, parish priest, or bishop, within his own sphere, and a general domination of clergy over laity would follow, as in Thibet; the Popes, however, claimed the right for themselves alone. Moreover there accrued to the Popes new and unlimited powers, exalting them over princes, peoples, and courts of justice, beyond what any mortal had yet enjoyed, from the so-called "Evangelical denunciation." It means that by asserting that it is a sin on the part of the defendant not to admit the right of the plaintiff, any cause can be brought before the Pope, if he chooses to meddle with it, — before a judge, that is, who is responsible to God alone.[3]

All roads at that time led to Rome. Whichever of the Isidorio-Gregorian maxims one started from, the result was the same. Either it was said the right of the Church is alone Divine, and therefore takes precedence of all other rights, but in the Church the Pope is the fountain and possessor of all rights, and thus every one is absolutely subject to him; or, the Pope is the ruler of souls, but the body is the mere vassal and instrument of the soul, — therefore the Pope is also supreme over bodies, with power of life or death. And again, whoever disobeys a Papal command shows thereby that he holds wrong notions about the extent of Papal power, and the irresistible force of Papal commands and prohibitions, and thus he incurs at least vehement suspicion of heresy, and must answer for his orthodoxy before the Holy Office.

The very names the Popes assumed or accepted mark the broad division between the earlier and new Gregorian Papacy. To the end of the twelfth century they had called themselves Vicars of Peter, but since Innocent III. this title was superseded by Vicar of Christ.[4] In fact the gulf between the position and rights of a Gregory I. and the pretensions and plenary power of a Gregory

---

1 Innoc. III. in c. 6, *De Majorit. et Obed.*, D. i. 33. Gregory VII. had before used the symbol of the two heavenly luminaries. *Ep. ad Guil. Regem.*

2 C. 13 *de Judic.* D. 2. 1. It belongs to the Pope "de quocunque peccato corripere quemlibet Christianum."

3 The chief authority is *Decret.* c. 13, De Judic. ii. 1.

4 Beugnot, *Scriptor, Rerum Gallic. x.* Prof. 47.

IX., or between 600 and 1230, is as wide as from Peter to Christ. All bishops had formerly been styled representatives of Christ, but when the Pope laid claim to this title, it meant — "I am the representative on earth of the Almighty, and my power stands high above all earthly power and limitations, in me and through me is the Church free," — according to the mediaeval clerical view of Church freedom, which regarded the Church as free only if omnipotent, and the Church in the last resort as simply meaning the Pope.

Gregory IX. went still further in his assertion of an absolute domination over the State, when he declared, on the strength of the forged Donation of Constantine, that the Pope is properly lord and master of the whole world, things as well as persons, so that his predecessors had only in some sense delegated their power to emporers and kings, but had relinquished nothing of the substance of their jurisdiction.[1] Innocent IV. claimed, as self-evident, the same direct dominion over the world, and all that is in it, only that he proclaimed in yet stronger terms the absolute universal supremacy of the Popes, and the union of the two supreme powers in one hand. He thought it false to say that Constantine had given secular power to the Papal Chair, for this it possessed from the nature of the case and directly from Christ, who founded a kingdom, and gave to Peter the keys both of earthly and heavenly sovereignty. Secular power was only so far legitimate as secular prices used it by commission from the Pope. Constantine had in truth only given back to the Church part of what was hers from the beginning, and what he had no right to hold. If possible, he spoke even more disparagingly than Gregory VII. of the origin of secular princedoms and their possessors. Innocent IV. supplemented the hierarchical organization by adding a link hitherto wanting to the papal chain, when he established the principle that every cleric must obey the Pope, even if he commands what is wrong, for no one can judge him. The only exception was if the command involved heresy or tended to the destruction of the whole Church.[2]

1 See Huillard Breholles, *Codex dipl. Frieder.* ii. iv. 921. "Ut in universo mundo rerum obtineret et corporium principatum."
2 *Comment. in Decretal.* Francof. 1570, 555. Innocent wrote this commentary as Pope. He has openly told us what amount of Christian culture and knowledge, both for clergy and laity, suits the Papal system. It is enough, he says, for the laity to know that there is a God who rewards the good, and, for the rest, to believe implicitly what the Church believes. Bishops and pastors must distinctly know the articles of the Apostles' Creed; the other clergy need not know more than the laity, and also that the body of Christ is made in the sacrament of the altar.—*Comment. in Decr.* 2. Naturally, therefore, the laity were forbidden to read the Bible in their own tongue, and, if they conversed publicly or privately on matters of faith, incurred excommunication by a Bull of Alexander IV., and after a year became amenable to the Inquisition.—*Sext. Dec.* 5, 2.

Boniface VIII. gave a dogmatic and biblical foundation to the doctrine of the universality of papal dominion in his Bull *Unam Sanctam*, where he condemns the independence of the civil power in its own sphere as Manicheism. He affirms that the Pope is judge over all secular matters where sin is involved, and holds the two swords, one to be used by himself, the other by kings and warriors, but at his beck and by his permission; that he judges all, but is judged by none, being responsible to God only; and that whoever denies this subjection of every human being to the Pope cannot be saved. His violent perversion of the clearest texts of Scripture in support of these claims was matter of astonishment and mockery even at the time.[1]

After the removal of the Papal See to Avignon, when the *Curia* had become French both in its *personnel* and its political line, the juristic dogmatism of the Popes was applied principally to the empire, and for centuries the steady aim of their policy was to break the imperial power in Germany and Italy and dissolve its unity. Clement V. declared "by apostolical authority" that every emperor must take an actual oath of obedience to the Pope, so that he might form no alliance with any sovereign suspected by him.[2]

The Popes even insisted to the Greek emperors and patriarchs on the undoubted truth of faith that all fulness of spiritual and secular power, at least in Christendom, belonged to them. Thus Gregory IX. and Gregory X. "We know this," said the latter, "from reading the Gospel." Innocent III. wrote to the Patriarch of Constantinople that "Christ has committed the whole world to the government of the Popes." And he gives, as conclusive evidence of this, that Peter once *walked on the sea,* — the sea signifying the nations, — *whence it is clear that his successors are entitled to rule the nations.*[3]

One of the most far-reaching principles gradually developed from the Gregorian system was, that every baptized man becomes thereby a subject of the Pope, and must remain such all his life, whether he will or no. Every Christian, even though baptized outside the papal communion, is not only therefore subject to all papal laws (though invincible ignorance may be a conceivable excuse in particular cases), but the Pope can call him to account and

---

1 See the writings of contemporary French Jurists and theologians in Dupuy's collection.

2 *Clementin. de Jurej.* Tit. 9, p. 1058 (ed. Bohmer).

2 Innoc. III. lib. ii. 209, *ad Patr. Constantin.* "Dominus Petro non solum universam Ecclesiam, sed totum reliquit saeculum gubernandum."

punish him for every grave sin, and this may extend to the penalty of death. For, in the first place, all disobedience to a papal command is either heresy or proximate herecy; and, moreover, the Pope can excommunicate him for his offences, and if he does not submit and receive absolution within a year, he is declared a heretic, and incurs death and confiscation of his goods.